Where The Guava Tree Stands

Leah T. Williams

Where The Guava Tree Stands

By Leah T. Williams

The Leaving

Sunrise washes Basseterre in hues of gold,

A final blessing, stories untold.

Mama folds the clothes with care,

Papa says, "A new life waits there."

I watch the sea, wide and deep,

Hiding secrets it dares to keep.

"Orlando, far," the whisper says,

"Will it love you in the coming days?"

The suitcase's snap echoes the room,

A future filled with unknown bloom.

Green cards clenched in trembling hand,

A ticket to another land.

Grandma's voice: "Stay bright, me child,

Keep your joy; it'll carry you miles."

Her apron smells of spice and thyme,

Memories sealed in the folds of time.

The monkeys chatter in the trees outside,

Their mischief boundless, their laughter wide.

Mama shouts, "Leave my guavas alone!"

They scamper away, quick as stone.

At the airport, my heart starts to race,

The workers move at a frantic pace.

"We're leaving now?" I whisper low,

Mama nods, "Yes, it's time to go."

The sea waves goodbye, a gentle sway,

"I'll see you again," I silently say.

Its voice is soft, a lullaby sound,

Whispering strength where fears abound.

Arrival

Orlando's air is hot and loud,

Busy streets and hurried crowds.

No guava trees, no ocean breeze,

Just concrete stretching endlessly.

The car smells strange, of leather and pine,

Papa's driving like it's carnival time.

Mama scolds, "Slow down, will you please?"

He laughs, "These roads too straight for ease!"

The house is big but feels so bare,

Echoes live in the open air.

Papa jokes, "Plenty room to dance,"

Mama's glance says, "Not a chance."

No cook-up here, no ginger beer,

Just snacks in plastic that feel austere.

"Where's the tamarind?" I ask aloud,

Mama sighs, "Lost in this crowd."

Unpacking feels like a strange charade,

Our lives reduced to what we've made.

The walls whisper "Who are you here?"

And I wonder if I'll persevere.

First Day

Classrooms buzz like a hive of bees,

Accents swirl like foreign seas.

"Say your name," the teacher says,

Eyes on me, like a predator's gaze.

"Mina," I say, voice soft, unsure,

My accent thick, a cadence pure.

Whispers ripple through the room,

A strange flower in strange bloom.

Their stares prick like burrs and thorns,

In their silence, my heart is torn.

But then a girl smiles wide, sincere,

"Hi Mina! Sit over here."

Her name is Chloe, her voice is sweet,

An anchor in waters fraught with deceit.

She shares her chips, her laughter too,

In this strange place, friendship grew.

She laughs at my jokes, "You serious, though?"

I grin, "Of course! Why, you didn't know?"

We trade stories, hers soft and tame,

I tell mine with flair, a story's flame.

Letter to St. Kitts

Dear Grandma, the sky here's vast,

But stars hide beneath a smoggy cast.

The food is bland, no pepper's bite,

No goat water to warm the night.

I miss the sea's eternal hum,

The way it soothed when days were glum.

Here, cars honk and engines roar,

The silence of waves I long for more.

Mama's tired; her eyes look dim,

Papa's hands grow calloused, slim.

They speak of visas, of papers signed,

Of laws and walls that bind the mind.

School is strange, but I've made a friend,

Chloe says she'll stick till the end.

She laughs at my tales of goats and sand,

Calls it a world so wild and grand.

She asked, "Do you miss your home?"

I laughed, "Miss it? I never feel alone.

Its spirit walks with me each day,

Through every twist and every sway."

The News

The TV's glow paints the night,

Faces grim, stories tight.

"Immigrants" the anchor says,

Words like spears pierce through my chest.

Mama sighs, her breath a storm,

Papa's fist clenched, his body worn.

The laws are changing, the risks grow clear,

Fear wraps tight like a shadow near.

I hear the word "deportation" fall,

A phantom pounding at our wall.

But we've done nothing wrong, I scream inside,

Why must hope and fear collide?

Papa jokes, "They'll need two trucks,

To carry all we've built with luck!"

Mama frowns, "Not funny at all."

But even I laugh at his bold call.

Guava Dreams

Dreamy guavas, ripe and sweet,

Dripping a tangy treat.

Under tree, I sit and play,

Caribbean sun warms my day.

Dreams dissolve in morning light,

Orlando's haze clouds my sight.

No guavas here, no sand shore,

Just echoes of things before.

I clutch my necklace, gold, small,

A gift from Grandma, my all.

Its touch is of home's embrace,

World of love I can't replace.

Mama teases, "you sleep long!"

Papa adds, "In dreams, you're strong."

I grin, "I'll bring guavas here."

Papa laughs, "mission clear?"

The Guava Tree

Papa brings home a sapling small,

"A guava tree, and for us all!"

Mama smiles, her eyes aglow,

"Feels like St. Kitts— watch it grow."

Soil is turned, the roots placed firm,

Hopeful effort with each turn.

"Guava tree in Florida, a dream!"

Papa grins, his voice supreme.

"Dreams take root in any ground,"

He says, his wisdom profound.

Though it's small, its leaves still new,

The guava tree feels like a breakthrough.

Seasons pass, the tree grows tall,

Branches stretch to shade us all.

Each fruit so tender and sweet,

A taste of home, a bond complete.

First Bloom

Papa digs, hands in soil,

"Tree please grow; and never spoil"

Mama waters carefully

Tiny seedling foreignly.

Weeks stretch long, the rains arrive,

Guava tree fights to survive.

Leaves unfold, a vibrant green,

Promise of all that's unseen.

"Mina," sings Papa in song,

"This tree is like us—it grows strong.

Roots do dig deep, branches rise,

Reaches the earth, dreams touch skies."

I watch it sway, the wind light,

Symbol of hope in the night.

And though the sea feels so far from here,

The tree whispers, "Home is near."

Carnival Memories

The drums would pound, people sing,

Streets alive with everything.

Feathers bright, in reds and golds,

Stories passed down, histories told.

Here, no carnival, no steel pan sound,

Busy streets, the world unbound.

I show Chloe what's back home—

"Your life's a movie," she says with a tone.

We dance in her living room,

She trips and laughs, "no costume!"

"You're doin' great," I cheer and clap,

She grins, "I'd fail at the map!"

The memories blur as days go by,

But Carnival's spirit stays high.

"One day, come, see the real show,"

Chloe nods, "You teach me, though."

Frayco Dreams

Chloe sips cold lemonade,

The ice melts, its flavor fades

"You've never had Frayco?" Why?

Shakes her head, wide-open eyes.

"Like a slushy, so much more,

Rich with sweetness, taste adore.

On hot St. Kitts days, cools your soul,

Bursts with flavor, makes you whole."

She laughs, "Fancy for a drink!"

I grin, "magic, what do you think?"

Frayco sunshine caught in a cup,

Once you start, can't give it up."

I try to recreate it, as best I can,

With crushed ice, syrup, and Mama's hand.

"It's close," I say, though it's not quite there,

The spirit of Frayco floats in the air.

Chloe tastes, her smile spreads wide,

"Amazing," she says with pride.

"It's a piece of where you're from,

Taste of home, Orlando's hum."

I nod, sweetness lingers long,

Bridge to home, where I belong.

In that moment, I feel complete,

Frayco's memory, bittersweet.

The Uniform Divide

"No uniforms here?" I ask in awe,

No crisp white shirts, no skirts without flaw.

Back in St. Kitts, we all looked the same,

Here, clothes feel like a fashion game.

Chloe grins, "It's freedom, don't you see?

Wear what you want, just be free to be!"

But I miss the pleats, the matching ties,

The unity found in familiar guise.

Back home, Form One meant a big start,

Each year a step through the school's heart.

But here, middle school feels in between,

A bridge to something yet unseen.

"Why no uniforms?" I finally ask,

Chloe shrugs, "It's just not the task."

But it feels like freedom traded for show,

A piece of identity I didn't know.

Standing in sneakers, mismatched hue,

A stranger in a world so new.

The bell rings loud, the kids disperse,

I walk to class, a silent verse.

Coconut Water and Cook-Up Cravings

Saturdays back home, the market alive,

Vendors shouting, "Come, take a drive!"

Coconut water chilled in a cart,

Cook-up bubbling, a rich-smelling art.

Here, no vendors line the street,

Just aisles of boxes, cold concrete.

I ask Mama, "Where's the cook-up meat?"

She sighs, "We'll make do, my sweet."

I sip from a carton, its flavor flat,

Nothing like coconuts fresh and fat.

Papa jokes, "One day we'll find,"

But the thought drifts, left behind.

Longing grows with each bland bite,

I miss the spices, the food's delight.

Chloe says, "Let's recreate your feast!"

I grin, "Fine, but I'm the Caribbean priest."

We fry plantains, the oil pops loud,

Mama watches, her smile proud.

The taste isn't home, but it's almost near,

A little piece of St. Kitts here.

The Game of Cricket

"What's cricket?" Chloe tilts her head,

I laugh so hard I nearly fall off my bed.

"It's not an insect!" I tease her grin,

"It's a game where legends win."

We head to the park, a bat in hand,

Papa marks the field, a dusty land.

I teach her to bowl, to hold the bat,

She throws too hard; the ball falls flat.

"You'll get it," I say, with a patient smile,

"It's about rhythm, not just style."

She swings and misses, her laugh a song,

But in her joy, I feel I belong.

The game stretches till the evening glow,

Papa joins in, his throw just so.

We cheer and shout, the world fades away,

In this little game, I find my stay.

Chloe grins wide, her hair askew,

"I love cricket; it's so much you."

I laugh, "Now you're part of the team,

A little taste of my island dream."

Mama's Market Day

Mama wakes before the sun can rise,

A determined look behind her eyes.

"We're going to the market," she says with pride,

"To find the flavors we left behind."

The stalls hum loud with life and spice,

Mama examines each grain of rice.

She finds a man selling fresh thyme,

Its scent pulls her to another time.

We spot a coconut stand at last,

The vendor smiles, his hands move fast.

The water is sweet, the taste divine,

Mama whispers, "It feels like mine."

Chloe tags along, her eyes wide,

"This is amazing!" she says with pride.

Mama laughs, "You've seen just a start,

This market is home, it fills my heart."

Bags in hand, we head back home,

A little less lost, a little less alone.

The market's warmth, a tether, a thread,

To roots that refuse to stay unsaid.

The Knock at the Door

The knock comes sharp, a chilling sound,
Our hearts freeze, no words abound.
Papa stands first, his voice steady and low,
Mama whispers, "What if they won't go?"

The door creaks open; two men appear,
"Immigration," they say, their tones severe.
Papa nods, his hand firm on the door,
"We've got our papers. You need no more."

Mama retrieves the folder thick,
Proof of our lives, every form and tick.
They glance and nod, their gazes cold,
Their power measured, distant, and bold.

"Thank you," they say, then turn to leave,

But the air stays heavy, hard to retrieve.

Papa bolts the door, his breath a thread,

"Stay calm, my loves; no need for dread."

I clutch my necklace, its warmth a shield,

Against the fear the knock revealed.

Mama's eyes meet mine, her voice so clear,

"We'll fight, Mina; we belong here."

Coconut Cravings

Back home, the coconuts would hang so high,

Their water sweet as the open sky.

Here, we sip from cartons stale,

Flavors thin, pale, and frail.

I miss the machete's swift, clean cut,

The fresh shell cracked, the coconut's glut.

Mama laughs, "We'll find some soon,"

But her voice feels wistful, a soft cocoon.

Chloe asks, "What's so great about that?"

I grin, "It's a taste you'll never forget.

Cold and clean, straight from the tree,

Like drinking the song of the Caribbean Sea."

We search for coconuts in a local store,

But they're hard as rocks, their taste a chore.

Mama shakes her head, "This won't do,"

So we make lime juice instead, something new.

Chloe sips, her face lights up,

"This is like sunshine in a cup!"

I laugh, "It's not quite home, not quite right,

But it brings a little warmth to the night."

The Talent Show

Chloe signs us up without a plan,

"It'll be fun!" she says with a waving hand.

"But what will we do?" I ask, unsure,

Her grin's so wide, it looks like a lure.

"We'll dance," she says, "something from St. Kitts!"

I laugh, "Do you know what that commits?"

Feathers and steps, the rhythm's a test,

But Chloe's excitement beats all the rest.

On stage, the lights feel warm and tight,

The crowd leans in, their eyes alight.

The music starts, my hips take the lead,

The beat flows through, a Caribbean creed.

Chloe stumbles, then finds her groove,

We twirl and sway, we find our move.

The crowd erupts, their cheers so loud,

I feel at home, strong and proud.

After the show, a girl comes near,

"Where are you from? That was so clear."

"St. Kitts," I say, my accent strong,

And for the first time, I feel I belong.

A Letter from Grandma

Dear Mina, child, how's your new land?

Are the streets big? Do you miss the sand?

Does the food taste right, or does it feel wrong?

Do the trees sway there, do they hum a song?

The monkeys still dance in the yard each day,

They steal the guavas; I shoo them away.

The neighbors still ask about you, my dear,

I tell them, "Mina is strong; she won't disappear."

Remember, love, your roots run deep,

Through every valley, every leap.

The green card is paper; it's not your name,

You're Kittitian first, a child of the flame.

Write me soon, tell me your heart,
Of all the wonders in your new start.
I'll keep you close, my pride, my star,
No matter how far away you are.

Love always, Grandma

The School Assembly

The gym smells like wax and sweat,

Rows of chairs, a stage reset.

"An assembly," Chloe whispers, low,

"About what?" I ask, "Do you know?"

The principal speaks, his tone is grave,

"Change is coming; we must be brave.

This country is built on those who strive,

Yet some question who should thrive."

I feel the stares, their quiet weight,

Like eyes probing, deciding my fate.

Mama's words echo in my mind,

"Stand tall, Mina, let love define."

Chloe leans close, her voice a thread,

"They're wrong, you know. Don't lose your head.

"I nod, my chest tight, my hands in a fist,

Determined to stay on my own list.

The speech ends with a call to stand,

For unity, strength, for the promised land.

But the tension lingers, like a storm in the air,

A fragile hope, a world unfair.

A Game of Football

"Football's not soccer," I explain to Chloe,

"It's a game of skill, where legends show."

She tilts her head, her brows in a knot,

"But Mina, that's what Americans got!"

"No," I laugh, "it's a Caribbean thing,

A game with a goal and a team's swing.

We play it on dirt, with bare feet wide,

Not on grass, and no rules to guide!"

We set up a match with kids nearby,

The ball's old leather, the stakes run high.

Chloe kicks wild, the ball veers off,

"Foul!" someone shouts, with a laugh so soft.

The game is chaos, sweat and cheer,

A slice of home brought over here.

When I score, the kids all yell,

"Mina's got skills; she plays so well!"

Chloe grins, "I get it now,

This game's a story, a sacred vow."

And as the sun dips, I feel the glow,

A thread of home in every throw.

Mama's Night Prayers

The moonlight spills through the curtain's lace,

Mama kneels in her quiet space.

Her whispers float, a gentle hum,

Words of faith when the world feels numb.

"Lord, guide us, keep us strong,

Help us know where we belong.

Shield our family, hold us near,

Calm the storm, dissolve the fear."

I peek from my room, her silhouette clear,

A steady beacon when shadows appear.

Papa joins, his voice a bass,

A duet of hope in our small place.

I tiptoe back, my heart a flame,

Their prayers a shield against the blame.

And though the world feels big, unknown,

Their faith reminds me we're never alone.

Chloe Meets Mama

Chloe comes over, her bag in hand,

Curious to see my homeland stand.

Mama greets her with a knowing grin,

"Welcome, Chloe! Come on in!"

She shows her the spices, the yams, the rice,

Explaining each flavor, each cooking device.

Chloe sniffs the nutmeg, her eyes go wide,

"This smells like Christmas!" she says with pride.

Mama laughs, "It's for more than that,

It's love, it's life, in every spat."

They cook together, pots bubbling high,

The scents fill the room, a lullaby.

"Your mom's amazing," Chloe declares,

"She knows her way with kitchen affairs."

I smile, "It's not just food; it's art,

It's how we keep home close to heart."

And as they laugh, their bond takes root,

In every dish, in every pursuit.

Mama whispers later, her smile aglow,

"Chloe's a gem, you should let her know."

The Neighborhood Cookout

The smell of charcoal fills the air,

Neighbors laugh without a care.

Chloe tugs my sleeve, "Let's go!"

I hesitate, but her pull says so.

The cookout's buzzing, plates piled high,

Burgers and buns, hotdogs and pie.

"Where's the fried fish?" I tease with a grin,

Chloe laughs, "It's America; dive in!"

A woman smiles, hands me a plate,

"Try some ribs; they're truly great."

I nod politely, but deep inside,

I crave Mama's cooking, the island's pride.

Papa joins, his laughter loud,

He chats with strangers, blends with the crowd.

Mama stands back, her eyes observe,

A quiet strength, her quiet nerve.

"Do you like it here?" Chloe asks low,

Her face lit by the cookout's glow.

"It's fine," I say, though my voice is thin,

"I'm learning to let this new life in."

The Letter to Grandma

Dear Grandma, the days grow strange,

The world feels big, and I feel the change.

Chloe's my friend; she makes me laugh,

But my heart's still home, split in half.

The neighbors are kind, their food is sweet,

But it's not the same as our St. Kitts treat.

I told them of guavas and Frayco's charm,

Of the sea that wraps you like a balm.

Mama's strong, and Papa jokes,

But sometimes the world feels like it chokes.

The news says things that make me fear,

But your words, Grandma, keep me near.

I dream of the monkeys, the tree-lined hills,

Of Carnival nights and quiet thrills.

I'll visit soon, I promise you this,

To feel the warmth of the island's kiss.

Love, Mina

The Soccer Tryout

"You should try out," Chloe insists,

"It's soccer, Mina, you've got this!"

"Football," I correct, my tone quite clear,

"Not soccer; we play it different back there."

The field is wide, the goals stand tall,

I lace my cleats, my nerves a wall.

"Show them your moves," Chloe says with a grin,

"You're quick on your feet; you'll surely win!"

The ball rolls close; I take my shot,

It soars through the air—straight to the spot.

The coach claps loud, his whistle a cheer,

"You've got talent; you're staying here!"

The team gathers, their chatter loud,

I find my place among the crowd.

Football connects, a bridge in my hand,

A thread of home in this foreign land.

Chloe runs up, her arms open wide,

"You did it, Mina!" she says with pride.

And for a moment, I truly believe,

That this new world has love to weave.

A Stormy Night

The rain pounds hard against the glass,

Lightning strikes, a flash so fast.

Mama lights candles, the power's out,

Papa hums softly, ignoring the doubt.

"Mina, come," Mama pats the floor,

We sit in a circle, the world a roar.

"Tell us a story," Papa suggests,

"One from St. Kitts, the ones we know best."

I think of Grandma, her tales of the sea,

Of mischievous monkeys and the tamarind tree.

I weave the words, my voice a song,

A melody of home, where we belong.

The storm outside fades to a hum,

Our laughter rises, warm and plumb.

Mama smiles, her face aglow,

"This is family, wherever we go."

And though the storm rages beyond the wall,

Inside, I feel no fear at all.

For in their love, I find my place,

A little island in this vast space.

The Teacher's Question

"Mina, tell us about where you're from,"

The teacher asks; my heart feels numb.

The class turns quiet, all eyes on me,

grip my pencil, my throat feels free.

"It's small," I start, my accent clear,

"An island where the sea feels near.

We have Carnival, cricket, and warm sunlight,

Frayco's sweetness, and stars at night."

The teacher nods, "That sounds so nice,"

But I see their questions, sharp as ice.

A boy whispers, "Is that in Spain?"

Chloe snaps, "No! Don't ask again."

I laugh, despite the nervous glance,
"St. Kitts is Caribbean, not France!"
The class chuckles, the tension breaks,
And my words flow out, the path they take.

"We wear uniforms, and school feels tight,
But the guava trees make it all right.
It's home, a place I'll always keep,
Like waves in dreams when I'm asleep."

The Green Card Worry

At the dinner table, Papa speaks,

His voice is strong, though his tone is bleak.

"The news grows worse; they tighten the rules,

Treating families like we're fools."

Mama listens, her hand on her chin,

Her fingers tapping, thoughts within.

"What more can they want?" I finally say,

"They gave us cards; we've done what they say."

Papa sighs, "It's not about us,

It's fear they stoke, creating a fuss.

But we'll stay grounded; we'll hold our place,

No fear will erase this family's face."

Mama adds, "Our roots are strong,

We'll prove to them where we belong.

Mina, child, your dreams will shine,

This is our journey, yours and mine."

I nod, though the worry stays,

A shadow creeping into my days.

But in their strength, I find my flame,

A spark of hope in the immigrant's name.

Chloe's Birthday Party

"Come over!" Chloe texts with glee,

"It's my birthday; you must come see!"

I wrap a gift, simple and small,

A bracelet I braided, colors and all.

The house is big, balloons abound,

The music loud, a party sound.

She greets me, "Mina! You made it here!"

I smile, her hug dissolves my fear.

The table groans with cake and treats,

Cupcakes, cookies, candy feats.

"No cook-up?" I tease with a grin,

She laughs, "Next time, you'll bring it in!"

Her parents smile, "We've heard of you,
Chloe says you're smart and true."
I blush, their kindness feels so bright,
A warmth that cuts the party's height.

As we dance to songs I barely know,
Chloe teaches me how they go.
We laugh, we spin, the night takes flight,
Her party a star in the Orlando night.

The Soccer Match

The game is set, the whistle blows,

The ball flies fast, the tension grows.

I sprint, my feet like wings on ground,

The crowd erupts, a roaring sound.

"Go, Mina!" Chloe shouts with glee,

Her cheer a fire that carries me.

I steal the ball, my heart beats loud,

Weaving through the rival crowd.

A pass, a kick, the goal is near,

I strike it hard, the path is clear.

The ball sinks deep, the net absorbs,

The team explodes in joyful roars.

Coach claps my back, his voice is proud,

"You're a star, Mina!" he says aloud.

But in my heart, it's more than play,

It's a piece of home in a foreign day.

Chloe hugs me, her grin so wide,

"You're amazing!" she says with pride.

And in that moment, the world feels small,

A field of dreams, a home for all.

A Visit to the Library

The library's quiet, a world of its own,

Rows of books, stories unknown.

Chloe says, "You'll love it here,"

I nod, though the silence feels too near.

Back home, books came worn and few,

Passed between hands, stories grew.

Here, the shelves stretch, endless and wide,

A treasure trove I want to hide inside.

I find a book with islands and waves,

Stories of sailors and hidden caves.

Chloe picks one with glittering stars,

Adventures on planets, journeys afar.

"Do you miss home?" she asks so soft,

Her voice a whisper, a breeze aloft.

"Every day," I say, my words a sigh,

"But here, I find pieces to get by."

We sit and read till the day grows late,

The pages a bridge to a shared fate.

In the library's calm, my heart finds peace,

A quiet escape, a sweet release.

A Taste of the Past

Mama finds a shop tucked away,

A Caribbean market, small and gray.

Her face lights up, her voice a song,

"We'll find home here; we've waited so long!"

The aisles are narrow, the shelves piled high,

With tins of mackerel, spices nearby.

Papa grabs breadfruit, his grin so wide,

"Tonight, we'll feast with island pride."

Chloe tags along, curious to see,

"What's this?" she asks, pointing to tea.

"It's sorrel," I say, "we drink it cold,

Sweet and spiced, a story retold."

Back at home, the kitchen hums,

The pot bubbles, the spices come.

Cook-up simmers, its scent divine,

A dish of memory, love, and time.

We eat together, the flavors sing,

A chorus of joy in everything.

Chloe smiles, "This tastes like art,"

I nod, "It's home, a piece of my heart."

The Citizenship Question

At school, they ask, "Will you be a citizen?"

The question feels heavy, where to begin?

"Do you want to stay here forever or go?"

Their words swirl fast, their meanings slow.

I think of the green card, its edges sharp,

Of borders drawn like strings on a harp.

Mama says, "This land's a chance, a start,

But home's not something you leave in your heart."

Papa adds, "We'll take each step,

No rushing forward, no secret kept.

Citizenship comes with time and care,

We'll decide when the moment is fair."

At night, I wonder what it all means,
The tug of two worlds, the space in between.
Chloe says, "You're Mina, wherever you stay,
St. Kitts or Orlando, you're you every day."

Her words hold truth, simple and bright,
A steady star in my shifting night.
And though the question lingers long,
I hold both homes, where I belong.

A Visit to the Ocean

Chloe insists, "You need some sun,

There's a beach nearby; it'll be fun!"

I hesitate, my heart unsure,

Will this ocean feel like the one before?

We pack a towel, some snacks, and hope,

Chloe's excitement helps me cope.

The car ride's long, the air smells sweet,

And then I see it—the waves that greet.

It's not quite St. Kitts, but it has a tune,

The waves hum soft, a sandy dune.

I close my eyes, let the salt air play,

Memories of home not far away.

Chloe laughs, "Come on, let's splash!"

Her joy breaks through like a sudden flash.

We race to the water, the tide's embrace,

For a moment, I feel this is my place.

But the sand feels different, the waves too tame,

Yet I smile and laugh just the same.

"This isn't St. Kitts," I tell her clear,

"But it's a piece of it, brought near."

The Citizenship Test Practice

Papa spreads a booklet across the table,

"We'll study this, it's time we're able."

Mama frowns, her eyes scan fast,

"This history feels like a foreign past."

Chloe offers help, her grin so wide,

"Ask me anything; I'm your guide!"

"What's the capital?" Papa asks her first,

Her silence is loud, her laugh's unrehearsed.

"I thought I knew, but now I'm blank!"

Papa chuckles, "You're just like a tank—

Strong and loud, but no direction."

We laugh, despite the tense reflection.

I flip through pages, questions galore,
About presidents, wars, and so much more.
"Who freed the slaves?" Chloe proudly declares,
"Mama, it's Lincoln!" I shout upstairs.

The laughter fades; the truth sinks deep,
This test decides the dreams we keep.
But we'll study hard, together, as one,
Our family's journey has just begun.

A Surprise from Home

The mail arrives with a package wide,

Mama smiles, "Look what's inside!"

I tear it open, my heart beats fast,

A taste of home, my memories cast.

Grandma's handwriting, her script so neat,

"A little something to make life sweet."

Inside are spices, bright and bold,

Nutmeg, cinnamon, treasures of gold.

A jar of jam, guava's delight,

And a scarf she wore on Carnival nights.

I press it close, inhale the scent,

A piece of love, her message sent.

"Mama, look!" I show with pride,

She holds it close, tears in her eyes.

Papa laughs, "She's spoiling us, true,

But this is home, stitched through and through."

We cook that night, the flavors sing,

The spices dance, memories spring.

And as we eat, the world feels small,

Home isn't gone—it's within us all.

The Classroom Debate

The teacher stands with a question bold,

"Discuss immigration—stories untold.

What do you think? Should borders stay tight?

Or should we welcome with open light?"

My heart pounds hard, a steady drum,

The room is quiet, my words won't come.

A boy raises his hand, his voice so loud,

"They're taking our jobs," he says to the crowd.

Chloe glares, her fist on the desk,

"Not true at all; that's just grotesque!"

The teacher nods, "Let's keep it fair,

Respect all sides, no room for despair."

I finally speak, my voice a thread,

"We're here to build, not to take bread.

Our green cards prove we've earned our stay,

We work, we learn, we find our way."

The boy looks down, his words undone,

The teacher smiles, "Well said, everyone."

Chloe whispers, "You were so strong!"

I grin, though my heart feels the lingering wrong.

Mama's Garden

Mama plants seeds in the backyard dirt,
Her hands are calloused, her feet in the earth.
"These won't grow like back at home,"
Papa says, watching her roam.

"Maybe not," she says, her voice so low,
"But I need something here to grow.
These peppers, these yams, this little plot,
It's all I have of the life I've got."

I kneel beside her, helping plant,
The soil feels warm, the sun's enchant.
"Will they thrive?" I ask, my hope unsure,
Mama nods, "Love makes roots endure."

Weeks go by, and green shoots sprout,

Mama beams, her joy spills out.

Papa jokes, "You've turned Orlando to St. Kitts!"

Mama laughs, "Just wait till the breadfruit hits."

Her garden thrives, her spirit glows,

In this small patch, her love still shows.

It's more than plants; it's life reborn,

A piece of home, no longer forlorn.

The Carnival Costume

Chloe finds a shop on the edge of town,

Feathers and beads, in reds and browns.

"It's Carnival!" she shouts with glee,

"Let's make a costume, just you and me!"

We pick out fabric, bold and bright,

Ribbons that shimmer in the light.

Mama helps sew, her stitches precise,

"Add a little gold," she says, "It looks nice."

The outfit takes shape, a work of art,

Each bead and feather placed with heart.

Papa claps when he sees me wear,

"Mina, you'll bring the St. Kitts flair everywhere!"

At school, they stare as I walk by,

The costume gleams, a butterfly.

Chloe joins with her simpler gear,

Together we shine, no room for fear.

The teacher smiles, "What's this about?"

"Carnival," I say, my voice rings out.

"It's joy, it's history, it's who we are,

A celebration that travels far."

The Protest

Downtown hums with voices raised,

Signs held high, demands amazed.

Mama hesitates, "Should we go?"

Papa nods, "We need them to know."

Chloe joins us, her sign in hand,

"Immigrants Belong" it reads, so grand.

The crowd moves forward, chants take flight,

A unified call in the fading light.

"Mama, will this make a change?"

I ask, my heart feeling strange.

She smiles, her hope a fragile thing,

"Every voice helps; every voice can sing."

The speeches start, the crowd leans in,

A woman speaks of the fight to win.

Her words inspire, her voice a flame,

She speaks for those without a name.

As we march, I feel the beat,

Of feet united on the street.

This is our fight, our future's song,

A place to stand, where we belong.

The Phone Call Home

The phone crackles, the line runs thin,

Grandma's voice breaks through the din.

"Mina, child, how is the land?

Are the people kind? Do they understand?"

Her questions tumble, her tone so warm,

A lighthouse glowing through a storm.

I tell her of Chloe, the friends I've made,

Of school, of laughter, and fears that fade.

"Do you miss the sea, the guava trees?

The warm island breeze that carries with ease?"

I pause, my throat catches tight,

"I miss it all, Grandma, every night."

She chuckles, her voice like a hymn,

"But you're strong, Mina, your light won't dim.

Carry St. Kitts with you, don't let it go,

Your roots will guide you wherever you grow."

Her words wrap me like a soft cocoon,

A thread to pull in the quiet moon.

And though the miles stretch far and wide,

I feel her close, right by my side.

The Neighborhood Kids

"Come play with us," a boy calls loud,

A group of kids forms a messy crowd.

Chloe nudges me, "Go give it a try,

You can't stay shy; time to fly!"

The basketball court feels strange, unknown,

The kids move fast, their skills honed.

But I take the ball, my heart a drum,

And with one swift move, I make a run.

They cheer me on, their voices bright,

"Hey, new girl's got game tonight!"

I grin, my nerves fade like mist,

In this moment, home doesn't feel missed.

Later, we sit, the game's long done,
Our laughter carries with the setting sun.
"Where're you from?" one boy finally asks,
His tone curious, dropping his mask.

"St. Kitts," I say, my voice full clear,
"It's small, but its heart beats fierce and near."
They nod, and in their eyes, I see,
A hint of welcome, a place for me.

.

Mama's Worry

Mama stares at the news again,

Her hands wring tight, her voice a strain.

"Mina, come," she says at last,

"Sit with me till this storm has passed."

The anchor speaks of laws that change,

Of policies cruel, cold, and strange.

"They'll target families," the reporter warns,

My heart feels heavy, my hope gets torn.

Mama sighs, "We've done all right,

We've followed the rules, kept out of sight.

But fear still lingers, a shadow near,

A quiet threat, a whisper of fear."

I hold her hand, small in mine,

"Mama, we'll be fine; we'll shine.

Papa's strong, and you are, too,

We'll face whatever we must do."

She smiles, though her eyes stay dim,

Her strength a flame, though worn and slim.

In her embrace, I feel the weight,

But also love that won't abate.

The History Project

"The project's due next week," Miss Hall reminds,

"Pick a country and its cultural finds."

Chloe whispers, "We'll do St. Kitts, of course!"

I nod, though my thoughts run off course.

We cut out pictures of Carnival days,

Steel pan bands and vibrant displays.

I tell her of cook-up, of cricket, of rain,

Of guava seasons and sugarcane.

She asks about history, colonial times,

I pause, the weight of those old crimes.

"St. Kitts has scars, but we made them bloom,

We built joy from a darkened room."

On presentation day, I take the lead,

My voice steady as I plant the seed.

The class leans in, their faces alight,

Chloe beams proud, her smile so bright.

Later, the teacher pulls me aside,

"Your story's strong; it fills me with pride."

And though my heart feels bittersweet,

I know my roots make me complete.

The School
Fundraiser

A flyer lands on my desk today,

"School Fundraiser!" in bold display.

Chloe asks, "What will we make?

Something sweet for old time's sake?"

Mama's grin spreads, warm and wide,

"Sugar cakes," she says with pride.

"Coconut, sugar, and a hint of spice,

Perfect for bringing a Caribbean slice."

We shred the coconut, fine and light,

Mix it with sugar till it's just right.

A splash of vanilla, the scent divine,

Mama stirs, "This recipe's mine."

The pot boils low, the mixture thick,
Carefully poured, each shape a trick.
"No oven needed," Mama exclaims,
"This is how the sweetness is claimed."

At the fundraiser, our table shines,
Rows of sugar cakes, sweet designs.
"What are these?" they ask in awe,
"A taste of the islands," I share with no flaw.

The treats sell fast, a roaring success,
The principal claps, "You've impressed the best!"
Chloe grins, "Mina, they love your sugar cakes,
You've brought St. Kitts to the school with grace."

As we pack up, the pride takes hold,
A little piece of home, bought and sold.
Mama whispers, "This was a sign,
Your roots are strong, they'll always shine."

A Walk with Papa

"Let's take a walk," Papa says at night,

The moon hangs low, its glow so bright.

We stroll the block, the air feels still,

The silence deep, the world uphill.

"You doing okay?" he finally asks,

His voice gentle, unmasking the masks.

"I'm fine," I say, though my words are small,

The weight of the day feels big and tall.

"Life here's different, I know it's true,

But your strength, Mina, will carry you.

This place is new, but roots take time,

Just like the breadfruit tree in its prime."

We stop by a park, the swings creak low,

The night whispers things I don't yet know.

"I miss it," I say, my voice so clear,

"The island, the waves, everything there."

Papa nods, his eyes like the sea,

"I miss it too, but here we'll be.

Home isn't lost; it's what you make,

In every step, in each breath you take."

We walk back home, the stars above,

A quiet moment, a father's love.

And though my heart feels split in two,

Papa's words thread hope through and through.

The State Fair

Chloe drags me to the state fairgrounds,

A place alive with sights and sounds.

"Funnel cakes, rides, and games to play,

It's America's Carnival for a day!"

The lights are bright, the music loud,

We weave our way through the bustling crowd.

I spot a booth with prizes galore,

Chloe laughs, "You're aiming for a sccre?"

We throw the darts, miss and miss,

Until the last one lands with a hiss.

The man hands over a bear so blue,

Chloe cheers, "That's all thanks to you!"

The Ferris wheel spins, we ride so high,

The world spreads out beneath the sky.

"It's not like home," I tell her there,

"But there's something magical in this fair."

She nods, her grin like the rising moon,

"Your world's a song, and I love its tune."

And as the night fades, the stars shine bright,

The fair becomes a memory of light.

The Unexpected Letter

The mailbox holds a letter today,

Its envelope plain, the print a gray.

Mama opens it with shaking hands,

Papa's beside her, tall he stands.

"It's from the government," she says with dread,

Her voice a whisper, her face flush red.

My heart pounds hard; the room feels tight,

Like shadows creeping into the light.

Papa reads aloud, his tone unsure,

"Just a reminder, nothing obscure.

Your green cards hold, but laws may change,

Keep your papers, and life arranged."

Mama exhales, her shoulders drop,
The fear subsides, but it doesn't stop.
"What if they come?" she mutters low,
"What if they try to make us go?"

Papa stands firm, his voice a flame,
"They'll not take what we legally claim.
We've worked too hard, we've built too strong,
This is our place; it's where we belong."

I clutch my necklace, its warmth a guide,
A tether to home, a strength inside.
And though the letter rattles my core,
Our roots grow deeper than fear's uproar.

The Rainstorm

The sky turns dark, the wind picks up,

Rain falls hard, filling every cup.

Orlando streets become rivers wide,

Cars crawl slowly, nowhere to hide.

Mama stares through the window pane,

Her hands are busy, but her thoughts remain.

"This reminds me of storms back home,

The way the rain would sing and roam."

In St. Kitts, we'd run when the skies broke free,

Splashing in puddles, wild as the sea.

Here, the thunder feels distant, strange,

The air is heavy, the mood deranged.

Papa lights candles as power fades,

The house glows soft, the tension sways.

"Mina," he says, "remember the hills?

How the rain would rush, and the world stood still?"

I smile, my memories flood with light,

Of warm storms drenching the Caribbean night.

We sit together, a quiet refrain,

As Orlando hums beneath the rain.

Chloe's Question

"Do you ever feel stuck between?"

Chloe asks, her voice serene.

"Like you're here, but part of you's not,

A place you miss, a home you've got?"

I nod, the words sit heavy and true,

"Sometimes, Chloe, I feel split in two.

Orlando's bright, but St. Kitts still calls,

In its rhythm, its spice, its waterfalls."

She tilts her head, her eyes so kind,

"Tell me more about what's in your mind.

What's it like to be from there,

And live here now, so far, so rare?"

"It's colors," I say, "so vivid, so clear,

The ocean's song always near.

It's guavas ripe, and sugar cane sweet,

It's festivals where the drums compete."

Chloe smiles, "It sounds like a dream,

A world alive, a living stream.

But you carry it here, I see it in you,

In your laughter, your stories, everything true."

Her words linger, a soft embrace,

A bridge between this and my island's grace.

The Carnival Parade at School

The school decides on a world parade,

Every culture a float to be displayed.

Chloe grins, "Mina, this is your chance,

To bring St. Kitts alive in a Carnival dance!"

We gather feathers, gold and red,

Strings of beads to crown my head.

Mama helps with a sash that glows,

"Wear this proudly; let it show."

On parade day, the halls transform,

Each float a story, each costume warm.

I walk with Chloe, our steps in sync,

The crowd erupts, their cheers the link.

"St. Kitts!" I shout, my voice rings clear,
Drums in my heart, the rhythm near.
I twirl and spin, my costume bright,
The island alive in Orlando's light.

The principal claps, the teachers cheer,
"Your float's the best; it's so sincere!"
And though the day ends, the pride remains,
A part of me here, where my heart sustains.

The Math Test

The test sits heavy, crisp and white,

Numbers and symbols blur in my sight.

I clutch my pencil, my grip so tight,

Hoping for answers to spark alight.

Chloe whispers, "You've got this, Mina,"

But math feels foreign, like Argentina.

Back in St. Kitts, we solved with chalk,

Formulas taught in steady talk.

Here, the questions twist and turn,

Graphs and angles I struggle to learn.

Papa says, "It's all just patterns,"

But my mind feels stuck in Saturn's rings.

The clock ticks loud, my nerves on edge,

I scribble fast, a mental wedge.

The teacher collects, her face unread,

I hold my breath, my cheeks turn red.

Later, Chloe asks, "How'd it go?"

I shrug, "I'm not sure, but I hope it shows.

"She laughs, "You're tougher than you think.

We'll conquer math over Frayco drinks."

And though the test looms in my mind,

I feel her faith, her laughter kind.

One step forward, small but sure,

A math problem's weight I can endure.

The Festival Lights

Mama finds a flyer taped to a pole,

"Festival of Lights," it reads in bold.

She smiles wide, her eyes aglow,

"This we must see; come on, let's go!"

The park is alive, a dazzling scene,

Trees wrapped in colors—red, gold, and green.

Papa buys cocoa, hot and sweet,

The warmth spreads fast from head to feet.

Chloe joins us, her hands held high,

"Look at the stars! They've lit the sky!"

We wander through paths that twist and shine,

Each turn a wonder, each glow divine.

A steel pan band begins to play,

Their music carries the crowd away.

I sway to the rhythm, my feet in tune,

The melody rising beneath the moon.

Mama hums softly, her spirit light,

Papa claps to the beat, his joy in flight.

Chloe twirls, her laugh so free,

"This feels like Carnival, can't you see?"

And though the festival is far from home,

Its magic tells me I'm not alone.

The lights remind me, through darkened skies,

Hope always glows where love resides.

The Green Card Renewal

Mama pulls out a folder worn,

Edges frayed, its corners torn.

Inside, our green cards, safe and snug,

A symbol of hope, yet a gentle tug.

"It's time," she says, her tone unsure,

"To renew these cards, to make them secure."

Papa nods, his face a mask,

Another step, another task.

We sit together, forms to fill,

Questions long, patience still.

"How long have you lived here? What have you done?"

The words feel heavy, each one weighs a ton.

I watch Mama write, her pen moves slow,
Each stroke deliberate, her care on show.
Papa mutters, "Proof of this, proof of that,"
Piles of papers stacked where we sat.

"Will this keep us safe?" I ask at last,
The words hang heavy, the silence vast.
Mama smiles, though her eyes betray,
"Safe is something we build each day."

We mail the forms, the waiting begins,
A game of patience, hope that wins.
And though the future feels unclear,
We stand together, holding near.

The Science Fair

A flyer hangs on the school's old board,

"The Science Fair's coming! Prizes assured!"

Chloe nudges, "Mina, let's try,

We'll create something cool, let's aim for the sky."

I think of home, the sun's fierce heat,

Solar ovens, a project neat.

"We'll show them how the sun can cook,

Using foil and mirrors, just take a look!"

We build the box, its angles precise,

Cover it with foil, shiny as ice.

Mama brings plantains, sweet and small,

"We'll bake these up, impress them all."

At the fair, our oven's a hit,

The plantains sizzle, their aroma a fit.

"Solar cooking!" I proudly say,

"Using nature's gift to save the day."

The judges smile, their clipboards click,

Our project earns a shiny gold stick.

"Mina, you nailed it!" Chloe cheers,

Her voice a balm to calm my fears.

As we pack up, I feel a glow,

A little piece of home on show.

The fair's a memory, bright and clear,

A spark of pride to keep me near.

Grandma's Call

The phone rings sharp, I grab it fast,

"Grandma!" I shout, her voice a blast.

"Child, how are you? How's the new place?

Do the people smile with kindness and grace?"

Her voice feels warm, a hug through the line,

Each word a thread, a stitch so fine.

I tell her of school, of Chloe's bright grin,

Of Carnival plans, where to begin.

"Do you still wear your necklace, dear?

Does it bring you strength, chase off fear?"

I clutch it tight, her question clear,

"Yes, Grandma, it's always here."

She tells me of the guava tree,

Its fruit so ripe, its branches free.

"The monkeys came, the naughty bunch,

They stole three guavas, their usual lunch!"

I laugh, her stories light the night,

A piece of home in Orlando's light.

"Come visit soon," she says at last,

"Don't let too much time slip past."

The call ends soft, my heart aglow,

Grandma's love, a tether I know.

And though the miles stretch far and wide,

I feel her close, right by my side.

The Spring Break Trip

"Let's go somewhere," Chloe says with flair,

"Spring break's coming—we need fresh air!"

Mama agrees, her smile takes flight,

"We'll plan a trip, something just right."

A park nearby, lush and green,

With trails and lakes, a peaceful scene.

Papa packs snacks, plantain chips in tow,

"Ready for an adventure? Let's go!"

The path winds long through towering trees,

Their branches sway in the gentle breeze.

I hear birds sing, their calls so clear,

A melody bright, a joy sincere.

We rent a boat, the water serene,
Chloe rows fast, her strokes so keen.
I laugh and steer, my heart feels light,
The sun warms us, golden and bright.

Mama hums, her voice a tune,
Papa jokes, "We'll camp here soon!"
Chloe grins, "I'll learn to fish,
And maybe we'll cook a local dish."

As evening falls, the stars take hold,
The world glows soft, its edges bold.
And though it's not the sea I miss,
This trip holds magic, a kindred bliss.

A Visit to the Zoo

"The zoo's amazing!" Chloe exclaims,

"Lions, giraffes, and all the big names.

"Mama agrees, "It'll be good to see,

How animals thrive, wild and free."

We wander through paths lined with green,

Cages and habitats, a curious scene.

The monkeys swing, their antics bold,

Their chatter reminds me of stories told.

"Back home," I say, "they roam the trees,

Stealing guavas with mischievous ease."

Chloe laughs, "I'd love to see that,

A monkey with guavas, cheeky and fat!"

The flamingos stand, their feathers bright,

Papa says, "They look like the Carnival night."

The lions roar, the sound profound,

A reminder of nature's powerful sound.

As we leave, I feel a thread,

A connection to stories Grandma said.

The animals here, though far from home,

Carry a spirit that makes me feel known.

The Immigration Visit

Mama wakes us early, the sky still gray,

"Get ready quick; it's a big day."

The appointment looms, a test of grace,

Immigration's office, a heavy place.

Papa checks the papers, a nervous hand,

Our proof of life in this foreign land.

Mama whispers, "Be calm, be clear,"

But the tension thickens with every year.

The waiting room hums with muffled sighs,

People clutch folders, hope in their eyes.

A name is called, a voice so cold,

We stand as one, a story retold.

The officer stares, her gaze a probe,
Questions sharp, her tone disrobed.
"How long have you lived here? What do you do?"
Each answer measured, steady and true.

Mama speaks firm, her voice like steel,
A shield of love, her strength revealed.
Papa adds facts, his tone precise,
Words that cut through bureaucracy's ice.

I sit in silence, my heart a race,
Watching courage fill this space.
The officer nods, her pen moves fast,
"Your cards are good; you've passed this cast."

Relief floods in, like waves on sand,
A fragile peace in a foreign land.
As we leave, the sun breaks through,
A brighter sky, a lighter hue.

The Soccer Championship

The field is alive, the stakes are high,

The championship game beneath the sky.

Chloe and I, side by side,

Our team's spirit, a roaring tide.

The whistle blows, the ball takes flight,

The crowd erupts, their cheers ignite.

I sprint, my feet a rhythmic song,

Dodging players, swift and strong.

Chloe calls, "Over here, pass it now!"

I kick it sharp; the crowd's a rowdy wow.

She takes the shot, the ball sails clear,

Into the net, the win is near.

The clock ticks down, the final blow,

Our team erupts, a victory glow.

We hug and cheer, the trophy raised,

A moment of triumph, a dream amazed.

Later, under the stadium light,

Chloe grins, her joy so bright.

"Mina, you're a star, a force so true,"

I laugh, "This win's for me and you."

And though the cheers fade with the night,

The memory lingers, a beacon of light.

The Family Celebration

Back home, Papa sets the table wide,

"Tonight, we feast," he says with pride.

Mama hums as the pot simmers low,

A smell of spices begins to grow.

Callaloo swirls, its scent divine,

Stewed chicken glistens with a Caribbean shine.

Papa slices breadfruit, crisp and sweet,

"Dinner's ready—come and eat!"

Chloe arrives, her eyes aglow,

"I've never seen a spread like this, you know."

Mama beams, "It's food with soul,

A little bit of home to keep us whole."

We laugh, we share, the evening flows,
Stories of St. Kitts, how the tamarind grows.
Chloe drinks sorrel, her smile grows bright,
"It's like Christmas in every sip tonight!"

The night stretches long, warm and free,
A reminder of who we'll always be.
Family and friends, a bond so tight,
A taste of home in the Florida night.

Under The Guava Tree

The guava tree stands, its shade so wide,

A place of calm, where hearts confide.

Mama sits, her apron tossed,

Her hands reflect the work she's lost.

Papa hums, his laughter low,

"Mina, remember how the fruits will grow?

Like us, this tree will take its time,

But patience turns to something sublime."

I sketch its form in my journal's page,

A tree of wisdom, defying age.

Its roots in St. Kitts, its trunk now here,

A bridge of love that draws us near.

Mama smiles as the breeze blows free,

"This tree will tell our family story."

And as the leaves sway soft and high,

I feel its strength, as dreams touch sky.

The Teacher's Praise

Miss Hall calls me to her desk today,

"Your essay stood out in every way.

You wrote of resilience, of finding your place,

A story of strength, full of grace."

I nod, unsure of what to say,

Her words feel big, a bright bouquet.

"You've captured the struggle, the quiet fight,

To stand your ground, to claim your right."

She hands me the paper, her smile so warm,

"Keep writing, Mina, you've found your form."

I clutch the page, my chest expands,

The words feel steady in my hands.

At home, I show Mama what I've done,

She reads it slow, her face a sun.

"Mina, child, this voice is strong,

It carries the heart of where you belong."

Papa laughs, "An author in the house, I see!

One day, your books will be read by me."

And though the future's a path unknown,

I feel my roots, my story sown.

The Storm Warning

The news says storms are on their way,

Rain and wind set to stay.

Mama prepares, her hands a blur,

Gathering things to ensure we're secure.

Papa boards windows, a hammer in hand,

"Strong winds can test any land."

I help stack water, the candles near,

The house feels ready, but there's still fear.

The skies turn dark, the thunder roars,

The rain pounds hard, the tempest soars.

We huddle close, the power goes out,

A world reduced to shadows and doubt.

Mama tells stories, her voice so soft,
Of storms in St. Kitts and their power aloft.
"The wind can howl, the sea can rise,
But love's the anchor that never unties."

The storm passes, the dawn breaks clear,
A calm returns, the air sincere.
And though the winds tested us that night,
We stood together, holding tight.

The Field Trip

The bus is loud, the kids all cheer,

"We're going to the wetlands—it's finally here!"

Miss Hall stands tall, her clipboard tight,

"Stay with your groups, and keep things light!"

The air is damp, the marshes spread,

Grasses wave where the waters tread.

"Look!" Chloe points, her voice in awe,

An alligator's head, its powerful jaw.

In St. Kitts, the creatures are small and sly,

Monkeys and lizards that dart and fly.

Here, the beasts are bold and grand,

A different kind of untamed land.

The guide explains how the wetlands thrive,

A balance that keeps the world alive.

I jot down notes, my mind alight,

Comparing this swamp to home's starlit nights.

At lunch, we sit beneath a tree,

Chloe grins, "This feels wild and free!"

I laugh, "It's different, but it's still a view,

Nature has its own rhythm here, too."

Mama's Job Interview

Mama smooths her dress, adjusts her hair,

"This is important—breathe, prepare.

"Papa nods, his smile calm,

"You'll do great; just bring your charm."

We drop her off, the building looms,

A place of desks and bustling rooms.

As she walks in, my heart beats fast,

Hoping this chance will help us last.

Hours pass, the waiting's long,

Papa hums a St. Kitts folk song.

Finally, she comes, her face aglow,

"They liked me—next week, I'll show!"

At home, we celebrate, small but bright,

A dance of relief in the kitchen light.

"This job's a step," she says with pride,

"To plant our roots and spread them wide."

Chloe's Family Dinner

Chloe invites me, her parents smile,

"Welcome, Mina—stay awhile."

The table's set, the dishes shine,

Roast and veggies, a feast divine.

"It's not as fancy as yours," Chloe jokes,

Her dad laughs loud, his spirit evokes.

"Food's about love, not just the flair,

And Mina's welcome—we're glad she's here."

I tell them of callaloo and spice,

Breadfruit roasted, golden and nice.

Chloe's mom nods, her eyes alight,

"Sounds delicious—perhaps one night?"

We play a game, we laugh till late,

A warmth that feels like fate.

And though it's not my family's cheer,

I feel at home, accepted here.

The First Sleepover

Chloe grins, "You're staying the night!

We'll tell scary stories, by candlelight."

I pack my bag, my heart unsure,

A sleepover feels like an untested tour.

Her room's so bright, posters galore,

Books and plushies cover the floor.

"This is my favorite," she hands me a bear,

Its fur is soft, its smile a flair.

We eat popcorn drenched in butter,

Laugh at jokes, our voices a flutter.

"Do you believe in ghosts?" she asks,

The question turns playful, behind her masks.

"Grandma says spirits walk the shore,

Guiding lost souls forevermore."

Chloe gasps, "That's spooky and neat,

But I'd scream if one stood at my feet!"

The night deepens as tales unwind,

Stories we share from heart and mind.

And though I'm far from where I began,

This friendship feels like part of the plan.

The Bake Sale Mishap

The PTA bake sale looms ahead,

Mama says, "We'll bake our bread!"

Sweet coconut buns, soft and round,

With a sprinkle of sugar, the best in town.

Chloe insists, "I'll help this time!"

But baking with her feels like a climb.

Flour flies, eggs hit the floor,

The kitchen's chaos from wall to door.

"Mina, how do you make it look neat?"

She's covered in dough from head to feet.

I laugh so hard, my sides are sore,

"This isn't baking—it's a kitchen war!"

But somehow, we finish, the buns align,

Golden brown, they look divine.

At the sale, they're gone in a flash,

One woman says, "These buns are cash!"

Papa grins, "Maybe we'll start a stall,

'Mina's Buns,' the best of them all!"

Chloe chokes on her laugh, her face bright red,

"That name might not be what you said!"

We laugh till tears, the day feels right,

A bake sale turned to pure delight.

The Soccer Fundraiser

The school announces a game to play,

A charity match to brighten the day.

"Mina, you're in," Chloe declares,

Her grin daring, her energy flares.

I hesitate, unsure, then nod at last,

"I'll try my best to run real fast."

Papa laughs, "Soccer? Not cricket, then?

Just score some goals and make a friend."

The field is alive with cheers and song,

Parents and kids, the crowd is strong.

Chloe passes, the ball spins tight,

I sprint and kick with all my might.

It's in the net, the crowd goes wild,

Papa beams like a proud Kittitian child.

"Mina, girl, you've got the feet,

For more than guava trees and heat!"

The final score reads loud and clear,

We win the match, the goal sincere.

Funds are raised, the kids all cheer,

A day of joy to close the year.

Mama's Promotion

Mama walks in, her face aglow,

"They chose me today; they let me know!"

Her words are bright, her voice so strong,

A step forward, a place to belong.

Papa hugs her, his joy a dance,

"Mina, this is what we call a chance!"

She laughs, "I'll manage the whole floor now,

No more taking orders—I'll show them how."

At dinner, we toast with guava juice,

Papa's jokes run loose and loose.

Chloe joins, her laugh a cheer,

"This calls for cake—or maybe beer?"

We all laugh, the air feels light,

A win for Mama, her shining fight.

I feel her strength, her endless climb,

Each success, a victory over time.

And though the journey's far from done,

Mama reminds us—together, we've won.

Mama's New Recipe

"Mina, taste this," Mama insists,

Her ladle drips, the air sweetly kissed.

"It's something new, but full of flair,

A mix of here and there to share."

Papa grins, "What's in the pot?

Smells like magic, hot and hot."

Mama laughs, "It's a secret twist,

You'll guess it soon, or it won't exist!"

The first bite burns, a fiery glow,

Pepper dances, steady and slow.

"It's spicy!" Chloe gasps, her face turns red,

"I'll need water—or maybe bread!"

We laugh so hard, our sides near split,

Papa says, "This one's a hit!"

Mama beams, her pride on show,

"I'll call it 'fusion,' a little St. Kitts, a little Orlando."

The recipe sticks, a family gem,

A symbol of us, a shining emblem.

Flavors of old, flavors of new,

In every bite, a story grew.

Papa's Cricket Game

"Come watch me play!" Papa declares,
His old bat polished, his spirit flares.
"They've got a team—Caribbean pride,
I'll show these Floridians how we stride!"

We gather round the dusty pitch,
Chloe and Mama, eager to switch
Between cheering and laughing at Papa's stance,
His cricket whites ready for the dance.

The first ball's fast, it zips through the air,
Papa swings wide, with skill and flair.
A crack resounds, the ball takes flight,
Over the boundary, a glorious sight.

"Six runs!" we cheer, our voices soar,

Papa grins, his pride restored.

Chloe yells, "Teach me that move!"

He laughs, "First, your grip must improve."

The match goes on, the game is tight,

Under the sun's relentless light.

Papa's team wins, their spirits aglow,

A victory sweet, like guavas in tow.

We head home tired, the day well-spent,

A reminder of roots and where they went.

Mama's First Car

"Mama, what's this?" I stare in surprise,

A shiny car gleaming beneath the skies.

"It's ours," she beams, her joy so loud,

Papa nods, standing tall and proud.

"We saved and saved," Mama explains,

"Now we'll drive through sunshine and rains.

No more waiting for buses to come,

This car means freedom for everyone!"

Chloe laughs, "It's sleek and bright!

Can I ride shotgun, just for tonight?"

Papa groans, "Who taught her that?

You kids and your slang—what's up with that?"

The first drive's bumpy, the streets a maze,

Mama clutches the wheel, her nerves ablaze.

"Relax," Papa says, his voice so calm,

"This car will take us far, stay strong."

We pull into a park, the sun sinks low,

The car feels like a new life's glow.

And as the night wraps us in its embrace,

Mama's car becomes our special space.

The Unexpected Guest

The knock comes sharp, an evening sound,

Papa frowns, "Who's come around?"

Mama peeks, her breath held tight,

"It's a neighbor, Mina, be polite."

The woman stands with a nervous smile,

"I've lived next door for quite a while.

Thought I'd stop by, say hello,

And maybe share what you'd like to show."

Papa invites her, his voice polite,

She steps inside, her eyes alight.

"This smells divine," she says with glee,

"What's cooking? Can I see?"

Mama laughs, her tension fades,

"It's stew chicken, rice, and lemonade."

The woman beams, "I'd love a taste,

Your flavors put my meals to waste!"

We laugh and share, the evening warm,

A bond forms quickly, breaking norms.

And as she leaves, she says with pride,

"I'm glad you're here, right by my side."

A Test of Courage

The school organizes a hiking trip,

"Nature's calling—get ready and equipped!"

Chloe cheers, "Mina, you're in!

It's time to sweat and maybe win."

The trail begins, the air is thick,

The path is steep, the rocks are slick.

I clutch my water, my breath runs short,

"Why'd I agree?" my thoughts retort.

Chloe laughs, "We're nearly there!

The top's a view beyond compare!"

Papa's words echo, "Push through, my girl,

Strength's like the sea—it'll unfurl."

At the summit, the world expands,

A tapestry of trees and open lands.

The wind wraps me, a warm embrace,

A victory carved in time and space.

We sit and laugh, our spirits soar,

"This hike," I say, "is worth much more."

And as we descend, my heart feels light,

The climb a metaphor for the fight.

The Surprise Package

A box arrives, its paper worn,

A treasure sent from where I was born.

Mama opens it, her eyes aglow,

"It's from Grandma!" she lets us know.

Inside are guavas, golden and ripe,

Spices wrapped tight, a tropical type.

A letter rests, its words sincere,

"Mina, I'm proud you're happy there."

She's tucked in photos, moments of grace,

The Carnival lights, the island's face.

Papa beams, "Look at these views,

The sea's as bright as the sky's deep blues."

I clutch a scarf, its colors so bold,

A story of home, a love retold.

And though the miles stretch far and wide,

This package feels like Grandma inside.

We feast on the guavas, sweet and pure,

A taste of St. Kitts, a feeling secure.

And as the night wraps us in its glow,

Grandma's gift reminds us, love will always grow.

The Unexpected Reunion

Mama reads a letter with trembling hands,

Her breath caught, her heart expands.

"It's from Cousin Ruth," she softly says,

"She's coming to visit—just for a few days."

Papa looks up, his face alight,

"It's been years since she left that flight!

She's family, Mina—you'll see,

The way she talks is just like me."

Ruth arrives, her smile aglow,

A whirlwind presence, a voice like flow.

Her laugh rings loud, her hugs are tight,

Her stories stretch into the night.

"I've missed this food," she says with glee,
"Breadfruit, callaloo, and tamarind tea!"
She shares her life, her tales unfold,
Of city lights and winters cold.

Chloe joins us, curious and kind,
Ruth's energy leaves her wide-eyed.
"Your family's amazing," she says to me,
"So full of warmth and history."

When Ruth departs, the air feels bare,
Her absence lingers in the chair.
But her visit reminds us, strong and true,
Family's a bond that time can't undo.

The Field Day Race

The school hosts field day, bright and loud,

Students gather, a chattering crowd.

Chloe grins, "Mina, let's race!

Show them your speed, give them a chase!"

I lace my shoes, my heart a thrum,

The starting line feels loud and numb.

"On your mark," the teacher calls,

The whistle blows, the moment enthralls.

I sprint ahead, my legs like wings,

The crowd erupts, their voices sing

.Chloe cheers, her voice a roar,

"Mina, you're fast—now push for more!"

The finish line nears, my chest takes flight,

I cross it first, the crowd's delight.

The ribbon snaps, my breath runs wild,

Papa beams, "That's my Kittitian child!"

Mama laughs, "We'll need a feast,

For our champion, to say the least!"

And as the day fades, the memory stays,

A win that carries me through life's maze.

The Community Garden Project

The school posts a flyer: "Volunteers Needed!

Help build a garden—the plan is seeded.

"Chloe grins, "Mina, this is for you!

You've got green thumbs; it's true, it's true!"

I roll my eyes, but I tag along,

The air feels warm, the crowd is strong.

Students and parents gather to share,

Shovels, seeds, and a will to care.

Mama joins, her hat perched tight,

"This reminds me of home," she says with delight.

Papa laughs, "Plant some thyme or peas,

Let these kids see what grows with ease!"

We dig the earth, its scent so sweet,
Soft as the sand beneath bare feet.
Chloe waters, her shoes soaked through,
"You're planting the flowers, not me too!"

By day's end, rows of green emerge,
A patch of hope on nature's verge.
Mama says, "Gardens teach us to grow,
Patience and love in the seeds we sow."

When the first sprouts rise, the joy is clear,
A little of St. Kitts grows right here.
And as the garden blooms and thrives,
So does the bond of our shared lives.

Papa's Work Story

Papa walks in, his grin so wide,

"You won't believe what happened inside!"

Mama asks, "What's the tale today?

Did you charm them with your Kittitian way?"

He laughs, "Not quite, but close enough,

You know these Floridians, not so tough.

They asked me, 'Where's St. Kitts, anyway?'

I pulled up a map—they were blown away!"

Chloe giggles, "Did they think it was fake?"

Papa nods, "They thought it was a lake!

I told them, 'It's paradise, pure and free,

Surrounded by the endless sea.'"

Mama smirks, "You're always so grand,

Selling our island like promised land.

"But pride gleams in her softened gaze,

Papa's stories weave love in subtle ways.

Later, I ask, "Do you miss it there?"

He sighs, "Every breath, like island air.

But here, we build, we grow, we strive,

A piece of home keeps us alive."

And though the day moves slow and steady,

Papa's tales keep our hearts ready.

The Cooking Competition

The school announces a new event,

"A cooking contest—show your talent!"

Mama claps, "Mina, this is for you!

Cook something they've never chewed!"

Chloe teams up, her smile so wide,

"I'll chop, you cook, let's show some pride."

We brainstorm dishes, the flavors collide,

"Let's make patties!" Mama decides.

The dough rolls smooth, the filling spice,

Chicken, thyme, and a dash of rice.

Chloe sprinkles, her hands a mess,

"This smells amazing—I confess."

The judges taste, their faces bright,
"Your dish," they say, "is sheer delight.
"We win third place, a ribbon shines,
But Mama says, "This win is mine!"

Later, at home, the patties gone,
Papa hums a familiar song.
"You see, Mina," he says with cheer,
"Home's in the food—we keep it near."

And though the contest fades from view,
Its warmth lingers, a flavor true.

Tea Time Reflections

Mama sits by the stove at dawn,

The kettle whistles, a new day's song.

In St. Kitts, it was fresh-picked leaves,

Bush tea brewed from the morning breeze.

"Mint, lemongrass, or ginger root,"

She'd pluck each choice like picking fruit.

But here, it's teabags wrapped in foil,

A far-off dream from Kittitian soil.

"Not the same," she says, her tone resigned,

"Tea was a ritual, a peace of mind."

Papa nods, his cup held high,

"I miss the smell, the open sky."

Chloe sips her cocoa beside me,

"What's bush tea? It sounds so free."

"It's nature's gift," I start to explain,

"A taste of the earth, a soothing refrain."

We laugh as Papa mimics the breeze,

"Drinking this here? It's like frozen peas!"

Mama smiles, "It's still a start,

Even if it's missing the heart."

And though the tea lacks the wild embrace,

We sip it slowly, finding grace.

In every sip, a memory stays,

Of mornings bright with bush tea days.

The Job Offer

Papa rushes in, his smile so wide,

"Mina, Mama, you'll burst with pride!

They've offered me more—a chance to grow,

A supervisor's role, I'll let them know!"

Mama cheers, her hands clasped tight,

"Hard work pays in this foreign fight."

I beam at Papa, his shoulders tall,

A little more space in this country's sprawl.

He sits us down, his voice sincere,

"This means long hours, but we're steady here.

We're building a life, brick by brick,

And now it feels less like a trick."

Later that night, as the house goes still,

I hear Mama pray, her voice a thrill.

"Thank you, Lord, for this day so sweet,

For strength to stand, for steady feet."

And though the journey's far from done,

Papa's victory feels like the sun.

A light that warms, a hope to keep,

A dream that grows as we fall asleep.

The Citizenship Ceremony

The day arrives, a moment profound,

Families gather, voices surround.

Mama clutches her scarf so tight,

Papa whispers, "This feels so right."

The hall is bright, flags on display,

Hope and promise light the way.

A judge steps forward, her voice sincere,

"You've worked hard; your place is here."

Hands raised high, we speak the oath,

A pledge of faith, a binding troth.

Mama's tears stream, her face aglow,

Papa stands tall, his pride on show.

My voice trembles, my words feel strong,
In this room, we all belong.
The applause erupts, the moment's sealed,
Years of fear and pain repealed.

The certificates come, golden and neat,
Mama kisses hers, her joy complete.
Outside, the sun greets us with pride,
We've claimed a home where dreams reside.

The Guava Tree's First Gift

A guava hangs, yellow and bright,

Its soft skin glows in the morning light.

Papa beams, his voice alive,

"Our tree has flourished, it's here to thrive."

Mama plucks it with careful care,

"This fruit is ours—a treasure rare.

A taste of St. Kitts in Florida's glow,

A reminder of how roots still grow."

She slices it clean, its flesh so pink,

The scent so sweet, it makes me think.

I take a bite, my senses rise,

Home and here blend, a sweet surprise.

"This tree," Papa says, his voice sincere,

"Stands tall because we're standing here.

It carries St. Kitts, it holds our fight,

Its fruit is love in every bite."

New Laws Loom

Even with certificates framed with care,

The TV whispers of laws unfair.

"Citizenship," Mama says with dread,

"Feels fragile now, like a spider's thread."

Papa nods, his brows pulled tight,

"The new government starts a fight.

Immigrants' children, they debate,

It feels like they decide our fate."

Mama folds the papers near,

Her movements slow, her face sincere.

"Whatever comes, we'll stand our ground,

This home we've made, this life profound."

At school, whispers echo low,

"Did you hear about the kids they'll show?"

Chloe says, "Ignore the noise,

Laws don't erase your joys."

But the fear creeps in, a quiet storm,

Uncertainty becomes the norm.

I hold my family close at night,

Bound by love, steadfast and tight.

The Storm of Change

The news spills warnings, laws in draft,

The future uncertain, the world's raft.

"Immigrants" they say, their tone unkind,

Walls of division fill their mind.

Mama's hands shake, her cup near spills,

"What if the tide no longer stills?"

Papa responds, his voice like stone,

"They can't erase what we've made our own."

Protests ripple through the air,

Crowds of hope, fear, and despair.

I march with Chloe, our signs held high,

"No human is illegal," our shared cry.

The chants grow loud, the streets alive,

A fight for rights, a will to survive.

Mama watches from the TV's glow,

Her face a mix of fear and woe.

Back home, Papa speaks with care,

"Mina, stand tall, show them you're there.

Your voice is yours, your life is too,

Let them see the strength in you."

And though the storm feels fierce and near,

Our family's bond holds us here.

Mina's Stand

The school calls for an essay to share,

"A moment of strength—show how you care."

Chloe nudges, "Mina, this is your time,

Show them your roots in a world of rhyme."

I write of St. Kitts, of waves and sky,

Of leaving home with a whispered goodbye.

I write of Orlando, a place unknown,

Of finding a space where love has grown.

I speak of fear, of laws unkind,

Of holding fast to peace of mind.

My words flow steady, bold and free,

A story of resilience, a part of me.

The teacher claps, her eyes are bright,

"Mina, your words are a guiding light.

You've shown us strength, the power of heart,

A lesson of life, a work of art."

And though the applause rings through the hall,

It's Grandma's voice I hear most of all:

"Child, your roots are deep, your branches wide,

The world is yours—stand with pride."

The End of the School Year

The bell rings loud, a final call,

Students cheer, they flood the hall.

"Mina, it's summer!" Chloe screams,

"Freedom's here for endless dreams!"

The year's been tough, a path uphill,

But I've grown roots, my heart is still.

Teachers smile, their hands held out,

"You've done so well," their voices shout.

At home, Mama plans a feast,

Papa jokes, "A summer beast!"

Cook-up simmers, the smell divine,

Breadfruit roasted, a Caribbean sign.

We sit together, the year behind,
A family's love, our lives entwined.
And though I miss the island breeze,
This moment feels like steady seas.

The summer stretches, a hopeful hue,
With dreams to chase, and time to renew.

Mina's Goodbye Letter

Dear Grandma, the days are bright,

The nights are calm, the stars alight.

I think of St. Kitts, the life we knew,

Its warmth still carries me through.

Orlando feels like home at last,

The fears we had are in the past.

Mama's strong, and Papa's proud,

We've built a life that feels allowed.

The guava tree you'd love to see,

It grows and sways, wild and free.

Chloe's still here, her voice a spark,

We dream of futures bold and stark.

Grandma, I'll visit when time allows,

To see the hills and pet the cows.

But for now, my place is here,

A home we've built with love sincere.

The Guava Harvest

The tree stands tall, its branches wide,

A symbol of hope and island pride.

Papa climbs with a practiced ease,

"Careful!" Mama calls through the breeze.

"You're not as young as you used to be,

Climbing guava trees back in St. Kitts," says she.

Papa laughs, his hand holds tight,

"This climb feels the same—my legs still right!"

He picks a guava, yellow and bright,

Its skin aglow in the morning light.

Mama shakes her head, a teasing tone,

"You'll twist your ankle, leave it alone!"

We peel the guavas, their scent so sweet,

Pink flesh glistens, the taste complete.

The Florida sun feels like Caribbean fun,

As we share the fruit, one by one.

"This tree," Mama says, her voice so calm,

"Grows from love, it's more than a balm.

It's our roots here, our dreams so strong,

Proof that home can stretch along."

And though the guava tastes divine,

It's the laughter shared that makes it shine.

Under its shade, we sit and stay,

A family woven in a new day.

Chloe's Farewell Party

Chloe's moving; the news comes fast,

"This summer's my last," she says at last.

Her voice cracks, her smile a mask,

Our friendship, now a fragile task.

We plan a party, balloons held tight,

Mama cooks, the scents ignite.

Papa grins, "We'll send her away,

With memories bright to light her way."

The house is full, her friends arrive,

Laughter and music, the night's alive.

We share stories, we cry, we cheer,

A bittersweet moment wrapped in the year.

Chloe hugs me, her eyes brim wide,
"You're my best friend," she says with pride.
"Orlando's bright, but it won't be the same,
Without you, Mina, and your island flame."

And as the night fades, her car pulls away,
I hold the memory of this day.
Friendships bloom, even when they part,
Leaving marks deep within the heart.

Mina's Reflection

I sit outside, the stars aglow,

Their light a gift, a steady show.

The air is quiet, the evening still,

A perfect pause, a calming thrill.

Mama hums as she waters the green,

Papa dreams of cricket scenes.

The guava tree sways, its leaves so free,

A silent witness to family.

I think of St. Kitts, its waves, its sky,

The way it stays, a lullaby.

Two homes I carry, their love combined,

A bridge of hope inside my mind.

"Grandma," I whisper, "you see me now?

Your wisdom lives and shows me how.

No matter where these feet may roam,

St. Kitts and here will both be home."

A Message from Grandma

A letter arrives, her script so fine,

"Don't worry, child, you'll be just fine.

The world's loud now, with storms untamed,

But remember your roots—they keep you named."

Grandma speaks of guava trees,

Of days spent weaving beneath the breeze.

"Even in Florida's foreign sand,

The island's spirit guides your hand."

Mama reads it aloud, her voice so soft,

The words lift like a gentle loft.

Papa says, "Her wisdom's clear,

We carry St. Kitts, so have no fear."

I write her back, my heart at peace,

Her words a balm, my doubts release.

"Grandma, we're strong, and though times are tough,

Your love reminds us we're enough."

Mama's Market Farewell

The market's alive, a bustling maze,

Rows of vendors, their goods ablaze.

Mama packs her stall with pride,

"Last day for me," she says, teary-eyed.

The move to Orlando brought her here,

A place of love, though never near.

But now her dreams take a new turn,

To teach and grow, to live and learn.

Customers stop, their hands held out,

"I'll miss this food," they softly shout.

Mama smiles, her strength aglow,

"This chapter ends, but more will grow."

Papa helps with the final load,

A bittersweet walk down memory's road.

And though the market fades from view,

Its lessons linger, steady and true.

A Visit Back Home

The tickets arrive, my heart takes flight,

"We're going to St. Kitts!" I scream that night.

Mama smiles, her eyes mist-clear,

"It's been so long, we need this year."

The plane descends, the island glows,

The sea greets us, the warm breeze blows.

Grandma waits with arms held wide,

"Welcome home, me child," she cries.

We walk through streets of memory's hue,

Familiar faces, the world we knew.

Papa laughs with friends from old,

Stories shared, their tales retold.

At the beach, the waves embrace,

A calming touch, a soothing grace.

"This is home," I softly say,

"Though I've grown, it calls my way."

And as the trip nears its end,

St. Kitts reminds us we'll always bend.

Two homes, two hearts, a love combined,

A future bright, deeply entwined.

Mina's Future

I sit beneath the guava tree,

Dreaming of what life could be.

High school looms, a world unknown,

A place where seeds of growth are sown.

Mama says, "Dream big, my child,

The world is yours, its beauty wild.

"Papa nods, his voice a guide,

"Your roots are deep, your branches wide."

Chloe writes letters, her spirit near,

Her words like laughter I still hear.

"Keep shining, Mina, you've got the fire,

To reach heights higher and higher."

I clutch my journal, its pages bare,

Filling it with hopes and care.

Of stories lived, of dreams untold,

Of lessons learned, both bright and bold.

And as the sun sets, the sky turns wide,

I know my journey is one of pride.

Two worlds I carry, a bridge of love,

Rooted below, soaring above.

A Dream of St. Kitts

The waves rise high, the moon glows bright,

I dream of St. Kitts in the quiet night.

Grandma's voice, a soothing sound,

The monkeys' chatter all around.

"Mina," she says, her hands so warm,

"Home is more than where you were born.

It's the laughter, the love, the ties you make,

The family you cherish, the steps you take."

The dream dissolves, the morning calls,

I hear the birds beyond the walls.

Mama smiles, her tea in hand,

"Sleep well, Mina? Dreams of the land?"

I nod, my heart a gentle beat,

Two homes merge, their blend complete.

St. Kitts and here, a perfect blend,

A life of love that will never end.

Chloe's Visit Back

The knock comes sharp, I race to the door,

Chloe's there, like times before.

"I missed you, Mina!" her arms pull tight,

Her laughter fills the house with light.

Mama cooks, the house smells sweet,

Chloe jokes, "Now this is a treat!"

We sit and chat, the hours fly,

Stories shared under the Florida sky.

"This feels like home," she softly states,

"Your family's love, it radiates.

Thank you, Mina, for showing me,

How roots can grow where love runs free."

And though she leaves when the evening falls,

Her visit echoes in the walls.

Friendships strong, no matter the miles,

Connected by hearts, laughter, and smiles.

The Bridge Between Worlds

Under the guava tree, I sit alone,

Dreaming of all the ways I've grown.

St. Kitts and here, two worlds collide,

Both a part of me, side by side.

Mama hums, her garden in bloom,

Papa laughs, his joy fills the room.

The future's bright, the past runs deep,

Memories treasured, dreams to keep.

I think of Grandma, her wisdom near,

Her words a guide, her voice sincere.

"You are both, child—root and wing,

A song that life will always sing."

And as the sun dips low, I see,

The bridge between worlds inside of me.

Home is here, home is there,

Home is love, a bond to share.

A Walk by the Lake

The lake winds gently through the park,

A mirrored world, serene and stark.

Mama says, "Let's take a walk,

A quiet day, a chance to talk."

The water glistens, the breeze feels cool,

Papa hums a tune from school.

I skip stones, their ripples spread,

A moment of calm, a path ahead.

Mama points to a family near,

"See them, Mina? Their joy is clear.

It's in the simple things we find,

A sense of peace, a steady mind."

We sit together, the world feels still,

The lake's soft lapping, a gentle thrill.

"This reminds me of home," I say,"

The quiet seas, the skies of gray."

Papa nods, "Home is where we make it live,

Where love resides and where we give."

And as we leave, my heart takes flight,

The lake's calm waters, my guiding light.

A Quiet Morning

The house is still, the sun creeps in,

A brand-new day about to begin.

Mama hums as the kettle sings,

The scent of tea, the peace it brings.

Papa steps out to tend the green,

The guava tree proud, its leaves serene.

I watch from the window, my journal in hand,

Writing dreams of this blended land.

Chloe's note lies open, her words so kind,

"A friend like you is hard to find."

I smile, my pen moves with ease,

Capturing moments like these.

The world feels balanced, steady, true,

A life of old and something new.

And as the morning turns to day,

I feel my home in every way.

A Family Dinner

The table stretches, plates aligned,

Mama's love in every bind.

Stew bubbles low, its scent divine,

Papa slices breadfruit, golden shine.

"Mina," he says, his voice aglow,

"This is our life, the seeds we sow.

From St. Kitts to here, through every strife,

We've built a bond, a stronger life."

Mama hums, her hands at rest,

"The journey's been hard, but we've done our best."

I smile, my heart feels full and free,

The weight of love roots deep in me.

Outside, the stars begin to blink,
I sip my sorrel, take time to think.
This house, this table, this family near,
Is the bridge of love we've made here.

And as the night wraps us in its care,
I see my two homes, strong and fair.
A part of me in each wide shore,
Forever linked, forever more.

A Toast to New Beginnings

The house is full, the air alive,

A family's love helps us thrive.

Mama pours sorrel, its color so bright,

Papa grins, "A toast tonight!"

"To dreams pursued, to battles won,

To all we've faced, to all we've done.

To St. Kitts, our roots, our pride,

To Orlando, where our branches abide."

We lift our glasses, the toast rings clear,

A celebration of a bright new year.

Mama smiles, her eyes aglow,

"We've found a place where love can grow."

And though the past calls soft and low,

The future beckons, a steady flow.

Together we stand, a family strong,

Rooted in love, where we belong.

Where The Guava Tree Stands

I sit beneath its branches wide,

The guava tree's shade, my constant guide.

The years have passed, its roots run deep,

Its trunk now strong, its promise keeps.

The air feels warm, the sky turns gold,

A story of courage begins to unfold.

Mama hums as she tends the green,

Papa laughs, recalling scenes unseen.

"Mina," Mama says, her voice so near,

"This tree stands tall, its meaning clear.

It's St. Kitts and here, its fruit and shade,

A testament to the life we've made."

I hold my journal, its pages filled,
Dreams I've written, and fears I've stilled.
Each leaf a chapter, each fruit a tale,
A life rebuilt, a voyage set sail.

Grandma's scarf wraps around my knees,
Her wisdom whispers through the trees.
"Child, wherever you choose to roam,
Remember this truth: love makes its home."

The world ahead feels vast and wide,
Two homes I hold, with equal pride.
From St. Kitts' waves to Florida's breeze,
I find my balance, my heart at ease.

As the sun sets low, the colors gleam,
I step forward with one last dream.
To carry my roots, to spread my wings,
A future bright with the song life sings.

The guava tree sways, its branches strong,

A silent witness to where I belong.

Two worlds I carry, their love combined,

A bridge of hope, uniquely designed.

A Letter to the Future

Dear Mina of tomorrow, bold and free,

Remember the lessons that carried me.

Home is a place that's built with care,

In laughter, in love, in moments we share.

Carry the island within your heart,

Its rhythm, its soul, its wondrous art.

But embrace the new, let your branches spread,

Build a life where your dreams are fed.

Mama's garden, the guava tree,

Symbols of roots and destiny.

Papa's laughter, his stories told,

A treasure more precious than gems or gold.

And as you step into the great unknown,

Know that you'll never walk alone.

Two worlds you carry, their love combined,

A bridge of hope, uniquely designed.

Keep writing, dreaming, and blazing the trail,

Through winds that howl and storms that wail.

Your story's yours—make it shine,

For you are strong, bold, and divine.

Acknowledgements

To God, who wakes me up every day, floods my mind with ideas, and gives me the strength to make them real. None of this would exist without You, and I am forever grateful for Your grace and guidance.

To my family, the ever-vigilant island-reference police, who never hesitate to remind me, "We don't say it like that." Your corrections are the backbone of authenticity—and your side-eyes are truly humbling.

To my cousin, Petisha, who refuses to let any of us give up on our wildest dreams (especially during vision board season). Your energy and big ideas keep us all reaching higher.

To Angela, whose creativity brings these stories to life with her beautiful book covers. You make my words shine brighter with your art. Thank you for capturing the soul of this journey.

To the brave souls I awkwardly asked to read early drafts—you didn't say no (even though I wouldn't have blamed you). Your support, kindness, and willingness to humor me mean everything.

And finally, to you, dear reader. Thank you for taking a chance on this book, for laughing, crying, and maybe even Googling "guava tree care" afterward. Your time and imagination bring this story to life, and I promise, the guava tree and I are both standing a little taller because of you.

Thank you!

Discover More of My Stories

If you enjoyed *Where the Guava Tree Stands*, don't miss my other novels:

- **Neither Out Far Nor In Deep, a** coming-of-age tale set against the lush backdrop of the Caribbean, where one decision changes everything. Also available as an audiobook for immersive storytelling.

- **Where Is Noemi?** A gripping young adult mystery about love, loss, and the search for answers that cut deep into family bonds.

Both books are also available on Hoopla, the free library app. If they're not in your local bookstore, don't hesitate to ask for them—it helps me grow as an author!

Visit www.leahtwilliams.net to learn more about these books and upcoming releases. Follow me on all social media platforms **@Kittiwriter1** for updates, behind-the-scenes content, and more.

Your next adventure awaits—let's turn the page together!